About
Skill Builders
Reading
Comprehension
Grade 7
by Jerry Aten

Welcome to the Skill Builders series. This series is designed to make learning both fun and rewarding.

This workbook offers a balanced mixture of humor, imagination, and instruction as students steadily improve their reading comprehension skills. The diverse assignments in this workbook are designed to enhance basic reading skills while giving students something fun to think about—from asteroids to the Great Wall of China.

Additionally, a critical thinking section includes exercises to help develop higher-order thinking skills.

Learning is more effective when approached with enthusiasm. That's why the Skill Builders series combines academically sound exercises with engaging graphics and exciting themes—to make reviewing basic skills at school or at home fun and effective, for both you and your budding scholars.

Credits:
Editor: Julie Kirsch
Layout Design: Mark Conrad
Illustrations: Jim Nuttle
Cover Concept: Nick Greenwood

D1291005

www.summerbridgeactivities.com

ISBN: 978-1-60022-147-7

Table of Contents

Suggested Reading List

Aiken, Joan
The Wolves of Willoughby Chase

Barron, T. A.
The Ancient One

Brashares, Ann
The Sisterhood of the Traveling Pants series

Cabot, Meg
The Princess Diaries series

Calvert, Patricia
The Snowbird

Choi, Sook Nyul
Year of Impossible Goodbyes

Christopher, Matt
Tight End

Cooper, Susan
The Dark Is Rising series

Corcoran, Barbara
Sky Is Falling

Dahl, Roald
Matilda

de Angeli, Marguerite
The Door in the Wall

de Treviño, Elizabeth Borton
I, Juan de Pareja

Eager, Edward
Half Magic

Field, Rachel
Calico Bush

Gannett, Ruth Stiles
My Father's Dragon

Gilbreth, Frank B. Jr. and Ernestine Gilbreth Carey
Cheaper by the Dozen

Gray, Elizabeth Janet
Adam of the Road

Haddix, Margaret Peterson
Among the Hidden

Henry, Marguerite
Brighty of the Grand Canyon

Hughes, Monica
Invitation to the Game

Jensen, Dorothea
The Riddle of Penncroft Farm

L'Engle, Madeleine
A Ring of Endless Light

London, Jack
The Call of the Wild

McCloskey, Robert
Homer Price

McKinley, Robin
The Blue Sword

Mills, Claudia
Hannah on Her Way

O'Dell, Scott
Island of the Blue Dolphins;
The Black Pearl

Paulsen, Gary
The Haymeadow;
Brian's Winter

Raskin, Ellen
The Westing Game

Seredy, Kate
The White Stag

Streatfeild, Noel
Ballet Shoes

Temple, Frances
Taste of Salt: A Story of Modern Haiti

Thesman, Jean
When the Road Ends

Travers, P. L.
Mary Poppins

Whelan, Gloria
Listening for Lions

Zindel, Paul
The Pigman and Me

Gold-Medal Miracle

United States Olympic hockey coach Herb Brooks knew that he had a pool of good, but young, hockey players as he watched them play during the tryouts for the 1980 team. He decided to choose the players who were the most aggressive and played the hardest.

Brooks was pleased with his final choices. However, he knew his team would be the underdog if they faced the powerful team of professionals from the Soviet Union (USSR). During the week before the Olympics began, the U.S. team played the Soviets in an exhibition game and lost badly, 10–3. In spite of the defeat, Brooks thought that if his team played up to their potential, they might be able to win a medal.

After the 1980 Winter Olympic Games began in Lake Placid, New York, the United States trailed Sweden 2–1 in their first game. With a last-second shot, Bill Baker tied the game for the U.S. team.

In the second round, the United States defeated Czechoslovakia 7–3. They defeated Norway 5–1 in their next game and then defeated Romania 7–2. A 4–2 win over West Germany followed. With a record of four wins and one tie, the Americans advanced to the medal round. Their opponent was the powerful team from the USSR. The Soviet team had a record of five wins and no losses or ties.

The Soviets took a 2–1 lead. Then, in the last second of the first period, the Americans tied the score. With 10 minutes left in the game, the Americans took the lead and held on for a slim 4–3 victory. Many sports fans consider this victory to be one of the greatest upsets in the history of sports. The U.S. team went on to defeat Finland for the gold medal by a score of 4–2.

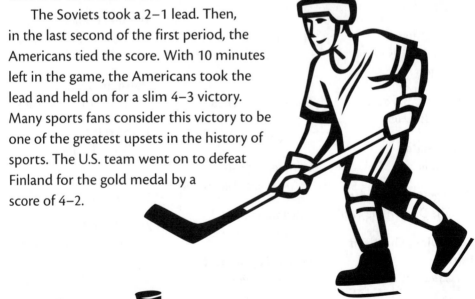

© Rainbow Bridge Publishing

Reading Comprehension • RB-904059

Reading Comprehension

1. In the 1980 Winter Olympic Games, the U.S. hockey team defeated teams from all of the following countries except
   A. the Soviet Union.
   B. Finland.
   C. Canada.
   D. West Germany.

2. What is the setting for this reading?
   A. Sweden
   B. France
   C. United States
   D. Canada

3. Which of these events happened second?
   A. The U.S. hockey team defeated the team from the Soviet Union.
   B. The U.S. hockey team defeated the team from Finland.
   C. The U.S. hockey team defeated the team from Czechoslovakia.
   D. The U.S. hockey team tied with the team from Sweden.

4. What was the U.S. hockey team's record in the 1980 Winter Olympics?
   A. five wins, one loss
   B. five wins, one tie
   C. six wins, no losses
   D. six wins, one tie, no losses

5. Why do you think sports fans consider the U.S. hockey team's victory over the Soviet Union's hockey team in the 1980 Winter Olympic Games to be one of the greatest sports upsets of all time?

   _____

   _____

   _____

   _____

   _____

   _____

© Rainbow Bridge Publishing

It's Missouri's Fault

Most major earthquakes in the United States have occurred in California and Alaska. Those earthquakes that have occurred elsewhere have been in areas with few people, and damage and fatalities were minimal. Since some of those areas have become heavily populated, there is a growing concern about possible future earthquakes.

The major area of concern is near New Madrid, Missouri, where four major earthquakes occurred in the winter of 1811–1812. Those earthquakes changed the topography of that area more than any other earthquake in North America. There were thousands of aftershocks, some felt as many as five years later. Each of the four big quakes would have reached a magnitude of about 8.0 on the *Richter scale*, which was developed in 1935.

The quakes in Missouri were felt around the United States except in the Pacific Coast. Large areas of land sank into the earth and new lakes were formed. The quakes even changed the course of the Mississippi River. The land where the Mississippi and Ohio Rivers meet was the most affected. Scientists thought that the earth's crust might have attempted to tear apart in this location due to the strength of the earthquakes.

The earthquakes destroyed many houses in the New Madrid area. Fatalities and property damage were minimal only because there were few people living there.

The probability for another major earthquake in the area is high. Scientists predicted a 50 percent probability for the New Madrid area having a major earthquake by the year 2000. That milestone has passed, and they now believe that there is a 90 percent chance of a major earthquake occurring there by the year 2040. A quake of such magnitude could result in a huge loss of life and billions of dollars worth of damages.

Reading Comprehension

1. What is the setting for this reading?
   A. Southern California
   B. New England
   C. the Southwest
   D. none of the above

2. Which of the following best defines the phrase *Richter scale*?
   A. a counter of earthquakes
   B. a measure of the intensity of earthquakes
   C. a way of predicting the possibility of earthquakes occurring in the future
   D. none of the above

3. What conclusion can you draw to explain the minimal loss of life during the series of New Madrid tremors?
   A. Few people were living in the area at the time.
   B. Better home construction and earthquake-proof buildings saved thousands of lives.
   C. People knew of the impending tremors and evacuated the area.
   D. none of the above

4. Which of the following was not a result of the New Madrid tremors?
   A. The Mississippi River changed its course.
   B. The largest of the Great Lakes was divided into two smaller lakes.
   C. Houses in the area were destroyed by the fault.
   D. The tremors were felt all around the United States except the Pacific Coast.

5. With the likelihood that the New Madrid area could suffer from another earthquake soon, what suggestions can you provide to avoid significant loss of human life and damage to property?

   I will make a bomb to
   brake a earthquake lane
   so it will stope releshule.

© Rainbow Bridge Publishing

Reading Comprehension · RB-904059

The First Burger?

We can't be certain who made the first hamburger or how its creation came about, but there is no dispute about the burger's popularity. It can be served flame broiled or char grilled. Some people love burgers buried in condiments like ketchup, mustard, and mayonnaise. Some top their burgers with lettuce, onions, tomatoes, and pickles, and there are some who like a slice or two of cheese, a few mushrooms, and maybe several strips of bacon on their burgers. Regardless of how it is prepared, a hamburger is the sandwich of choice for many people.

Residents of Seymour, Wisconsin, argue that Charlie Nagreen created the first hamburger in 1885, when he was only 15 years old. Charlie was selling meatballs at a concession stand at the Outagamie County Fair. He watched people and decided that meatballs were too difficult for them to eat while walking around the fair. Charlie flattened the meatballs, placed them between two slices of bread, and called his creation a "hamburger."

People in Stark County, Ohio, think that Frank Menches invented the first burger. He was working in a concession stand at a county fair in the 1880s. Menches ran out of pork for his sausage-patty sandwiches. He used beef in place of pork and called the sandwich a "hamburger" in honor of the town Hamburg, New York, where the fair was held.

Then, there are Texans who claim that the first burger was made by Fletcher Davis of Athens, Texas. Davis placed raw beef on his grill, cooked it, and placed it between two slices of homemade toast. He added a slice of raw onion on top. It was so popular that his friends urged him to open a concession stand. He and his wife, Ciddy, followed their advice and made his sandwich famous at the 1904 World's Fair in St. Louis.

There are more stories of how the hamburger was invented. However, we don't have to know whose idea it was to know that it was a good one!

dispute
argue

© Rainbow Bridge Publishing

Reading Comprehension

1. Which of the following would be the best title for this reading?
   A. Inventions at the World's Fair B. Hamburger History
   C. Creative Cooking   D. Cheeseburgers in Paradise

2. Which of these conclusions can you draw from the reading?
   A. Ray Kroc built an empire under his golden arches.
   B. Frank Menches probably created the first hamburger.
   C. We don't know who invented the hamburger.
   D. The claim that Fletcher Davis created the first burger is the most plausible.

3. Which of these statements is true?
   A. The Outagamie County Fair was held every year in Michigan.
   B. Frank Menches named his hamburger in honor of Hamburg, New York.
   C. Fletcher Davis served his sandwich raw.
   D. Cheeseburgers should always be grilled on only one side to prevent the cheese from burning.

4. Which of the following best defines the word *condiment*?
   A. something used to enhance flavor
   B. a license required for all street vendors
   C. a substitute for raw meat
   D. none of the above

5. Describe your favorite burger or sandwich. What do you put on it? Which restaurant do you think makes the best burger or sandwich?

   I like chicken sandwich. And
   I like Hope plaen and have
   Bodolo sas it realy hot.
   is

© Rainbow Bridge Publishing   *Reading Comprehension* • RB-904059

Analyzing Poetry

Although Emily Dickinson is now one of the most famous American poets of all time, she was virtually unknown during her lifetime. Of the approximately 1,800 poems that she wrote, only seven were published during her lifetime. Today, Dickinson is known for her unusual use of capital letters and punctuation, vivid imagery, slant rhyme, and broken meter. She did not give her poems titles. Instead, Dickinson's poems are often organized in chronological order and assigned a number based on when scholars think that each poem was written.

254
"Hope" is the thing with feathers –
That perches in the soul –
And sings the tune without the words –
And never stops – at all –

And sweetest – in the Gale – is heard –
And sore must be the storm –
That could *abash* the little Bird
That kept so many warm –

I've heard it in the chillest land –
And on the strangest Sea –
Yet, never, in Extremity,
It asked a crumb – of Me.

© Rainbow Bridge Publishing   *Reading Comprehension* • RB-904059

Reading Comprehension

1. To what does Emily Dickinson compare hope?
   - A. a song
   - B. a bird
   - C. a strong wind
   - D. all of the above

2. Which of the following best defines the word *abash*?
   - A. to frighten into silence
   - B. to freeze or chill
   - C. to wound or injure
   - D. to unsettle or embarrass

3. What do you think Dickinson means when she writes that hope is "sweetest - in the Gale?"

   _____

   _____

   _____

4. When words sound the same but do not rhyme exactly, they are called slant rhymes. Find two pairs of slant rhymes in the poem and write them in the spaces below.

   _____ / _____

   _____ / _____

5. Dickinson is famous for her sporadic use of dashes and punctuation, slant rhymes, unusual capitalization, and broken meter. How do these characteristics affect the way you read the poem?

   _____

   _____

   _____

   _____

Fabulous Fables

A fable is a short story that teaches a specific lesson. This lesson can often be summarized in a single sentence. An example of a fable's moral is "Look before you leap," which means that you should always consider the consequences of an action. Aesop, a Greek man who lived around 600 BC, is famous for his many fables.

The following fables are based on Aesop's fables. Read each fable. Then, in one sentence, summarize the fable's lesson.

1. A Lion was awakened by a Mouse running over his face. Rising in anger, he caught the Mouse and was about to kill him when the Mouse said, "If you would only spare my life, I would be sure to repay your kindness." The Lion laughed and let the Mouse go. It happened shortly after this that the Lion was caught by some hunters, who bound him to the ground with strong ropes. The Mouse, recognizing the Lion's roar, came up and gnawed the rope with his teeth, and, setting the Lion free, exclaimed, "You ridiculed the idea of me ever being able to help you, not expecting to receive from me any repayment of your favor, but now you know that it is possible for even a Mouse to help a Lion."

    _____

2. The North Wind and the Sun disputed who was more powerful and agreed that he who could first strip a wayfaring man of his clothes should be declared the victor. The North Wind tried his power first and blew with all of his might. But, the keener his blasts became, the closer the traveler wrapped his cloak around himself. At last, resigning all hope of victory, the North Wind called upon the Sun to see what he could do. The Sun suddenly shone out with all of his warmth. The traveler no sooner felt the Sun's genial rays than he took off one garment after another. At last, fairly overcome with heat, the traveler undressed and bathed in a stream that lay in his path.

    _____

© Rainbow Bridge Publishing

Reading Comprehension • RB-904059

Fabulous Fables (continued)

3. A thirsty Crow came upon a pitcher that had once been full of water. When the Crow put his beak into the mouth of the pitcher, he found that it now held very little water. He could not reach his beak far enough into the pitcher to take a drink. Though he tried and tried, he could not reach the water. Then, a thought came to him, and he took a pebble and dropped it into the pitcher. He took another pebble and dropped it into the pitcher. He dropped pebble after pebble into the pitcher. With each pebble, the water rose slightly. At last, he saw the water rise near the top of the pitcher. After casting in a few more pebbles, he was able to quench his thirst.

    _____

4. A Dog had found a piece of meat and was carrying it home in his mouth to eat it in peace. On his way home, he had to cross a wooden plank that was lying across a swiftly running stream. As he crossed, he looked down and saw his reflection in the water. Thinking it was another dog with another piece of meat, he made up his mind to have both pieces of meat. He snapped at his reflection, but as he opened his mouth the piece of meat fell out, dropped into the water, and was never seen again.

    _____

5. An old man summoned his sons around him to give them some advice. He asked his servants to bring in a bundle of sticks and said to his oldest son, "Break it." The son strained and strained, but he was unable to break the bundle. The other sons also tried, but none of them was successful. "Untie the sticks," said the father, "and each of you take a stick." When they had done so, he said to them, "Now, break the sticks," and each stick was easily broken. "You see my meaning," said their father.

    _____

© Rainbow Bridge Publishing

Reading Comprehension • RB-904059

On the Mission Trail

When Columbus landed in the New World, Spain began claiming much of North America. Juan Rodríguez Cabrillo explored the Pacific Coast when he sailed from Mexico in 1542.

In 1602, Sebastían Vizcaíno also explored the California coast, and he urged Spain to colonize the area. In 1697, Jesuit missions began springing up in Baja, California. However, King Carlos III of Spain expelled the Jesuit missionaries from Baja because he thought they were not sending him his share of the gold that was discovered there.

The priest who took over the Jesuit missions in 1767 was Junípero Serra. He sent word to Spain that Russians were building fur-trading posts in northern California. The Spanish king became concerned.

The king sent priests and soldiers to build a trail of missions. The soldiers were also sent to protect the missions. The missions were inexpensive because they were self-sufficient. The priests received no pay, and they had few needs.

The priests were followers of St. Francis of Assisi. Their goal was to convert the Native Americans to Christianity. The missions were appealing to Spain, because they kept the land under Spanish control. The first mission in the trail was built in San Diego in 1769.

A chain of 21 missions was built along California's El Camino Real ("The King's Highway"). It extended from San Diego to San Francisco. Missions were located a day's walk from each other. In addition to converting Native Americans to Christianity, the missions brought industry, livestock, and

the cultivation of fruits, flowers, and grains to California. The missions were a significant factor in the early colonization of California and the strengthening of its Spanish heritage.

© Rainbow Bridge Publishing

Reading Comprehension

1. Which of the following best explains the Spanish crown's establishment of missions in California?
   A. its desire to convert the Native Americans to Christianity
   B. the need to colonize the area
   C. the expansion of the citrus fruit industry
   D. the desire to help migrant workers find their own land

2. Why did the Spanish king expel the Jesuit missionaries?
   A. He preferred the followers of St. Francis of Assisi to the Jesuits.
   B. He thought that the missionaries were not sending him his share of the gold.
   C. He wanted to establish a more aggressive colony of Christians.
   D. He felt the missions would be better built by Franciscan construction workers.

3. Which of these events did not happen?
   A. Russia established trading posts in northern California.
   B. Christopher Columbus fell in love with California at first sight.
   C. A chain of 21 Spanish missions was built between San Diego and San Francisco.
   D. Priests and soldiers built a trail of missions extending from San Diego to San Francisco.

4. The Spanish king was willing to establish the chain of missions in California because:
   A. They were inexpensive to maintain.
   B. He felt that they would protect Spanish claims in the area.
   C. He felt that their presence would deter Russians from extending their settlements farther south.
   D. all of the above

5. What role did the mission trail play in the early history of California?

   _____

   _____

© Rainbow Bridge Publishing   *Reading Comprehension* • RB-904059

Seventh-Inning Stretch

The seventh-inning stretch is one baseball tradition that helps make the game one of America's favorite pastimes. In the middle of the seventh inning, fans *ritualistically* stand and stretch before the home team comes to bat.

No one really knows the origin of the custom, but there are theories on how it started. Baseball historian Dan Daniel provided this explanation: "It probably began as an expression of fatigue. That would explain why the stretch comes late in the game instead of at the halfway point."

A more popular story involves President William Howard Taft and the birth of two baseball traditions. According to the account, Taft attended the first game of the 1910 baseball season. On the spur of the moment, plate umpire Billy Evans gave Taft the ball. He asked him to throw it over the plate. Taft did so, and the custom of having the president launch the baseball season with the first pitch was born.

The story continues that later that same day, President Taft, who weighed well over 300 pounds, became uncomfortable in his small chair. In the middle of the seventh inning, he stood up to stretch his legs. The crowd thought that the president was leaving, so they stood up out of respect. A few moments later, Taft sat down again. The fans followed, and the seventh-inning stretch was born. What a day for traditions!

No matter how the tradition began, fans have since added to the fun. Now, as they stand to stretch during the seventh inning, they can sing along to Jack Norworth's 1927 version of the song "Take Me Out to the Ball Game" after the visiting team has batted.

Reading Comprehension

1. Which of the following best best defines the word *ritualistically*?
   A. excessively devoted
   B. duty bound
   C. continuing a custom
   D. released from liability

2. When is the seventh-inning stretch celebrated with the song "Take Me Out to the Ball Game"?
   A. between the sixth and seventh innings
   B. after the visiting team has batted in the seventh inning
   C. after the home team has batted in the seventh inning
   D. none of the above

3. How did the custom of observing the "seventh-inning stretch" begin?
   A. Fans used it as a time to stand and stretch their legs after sitting for the first six innings.
   B. William Howard Taft got tired of sitting in his cramped wooden chair, so he stood up and the rest of the fans stood in honor of the president.
   C. No one knows for sure where or when the custom began.
   D. Jack Norworth started the tradition in 1927.

4. Who was Billy Evans?
   A. the catcher who tossed the ball to President Taft
   B. the pitcher who asked President Taft to throw the ball back to him
   C. the plate umpire who gave the ball to President Taft
   D. the stadium announcer

5. Why do you think the seventh inning was chosen to stand, stretch, and "root for the home team" rather than some other inning?

_____

_____

_____

_____

© Rainbow Bridge Publishing Reading Comprehension • RB-904059

Sunshine in Seattle

Most people who live in Seattle, Washington, love their city. There is a never-ending flow of fun things to do. But, people who live there do not always enjoy the day-after-day absence of sunshine during the winter months.

It is a documented fact that sunshine (or lack of it) plays a major role in how each of us meets the day. It also affects how we perform at school or work. When people are deprived of sunlight, they can develop *seasonal affective disorder*, which makes it difficult for them to feel happy or get things accomplished. No major city in the United States is more affected by the "sunshine factor" than Seattle.

To combat drizzle and fog during the winter months, Steve Murphy created a business that is very popular among the locals. The Indoor Sun Shoppe is more than a little ray of sunshine during the gray days of Seattle's winter. His shop offers a huge source of plants and artificial lighting for people who are trying to overcome seasonal affective disorder.

Located in Fremont, Washington, The Indoor Sun Shoppe has an amazing collection of exotic plants and "good bugs" in a humid and well-lit environment. At The Indoor Sun Shoppe, you can spend up to $400 for artificial lighting that will chase away the winter blues. It will also keep your plants healthy. You can buy a dawn simulator that will gradually fill your room with a warming wake-up glow. What better way to meet a Seattle morning when real sunshine is nothing more than a happy thought!

Murphy's in-home waterfalls are also popular with customers. But his plants and lights remain the "main course." On a cloudy winter day, The Indoor Sun Shoppe is a bright spot in Seattle!

Reading Comprehension

1. Which of these statements is false?
   A. Seattle is located in the state of Washington.
   B. Sunshine in Seattle is rare during the winter months.
   C. Some people who live in Seattle suffer from seasonal affective disorder.
   D. None of the above.

2. Judging from the reading, some suggestions for beating the winter blues include all of the following except
   A. keeping a lot of plants in your home environment.
   B. having plenty of artificial lighting in your home.
   C. installing in-home waterfalls to bring the outdoors into your home.
   D. using tanning beds to soak up the Seattle sunshine.

3. Which of the following best defines the term *seasonal affective disorder*?
   A. lethargy, depression, and lack of energy caused by a lack of sunlight
   B. mild temperature, coughing, and a general feeling of illness
   C. winter-related illness caused by spending too much time outside
   D. post-holiday depression that comes when relatives leave

4. Which of the following best explains the use of a dawn simulator?
   A. an alarm clock stimulated by the light rays of early morning
   B. a bringer of indoor sunshine when there is none outside
   C. an automatic sprinkling system for indoor plants
   D. a healthy alternative to tanning beds

© Rainbow Bridge Publishing *Reading Comprehension* • RB-904059

The Last Spike

The Last Spike was also known as the Golden Spike. It was the final link in the first transcontinental railroad across the United States. California Governor Leland Stanford tapped the spike into place on May 10, 1869. The spike joined the Central Pacific and Union Pacific Railroads.

Between the settlements in the Midwest and those in the far West, there were more than 1,500 miles (2,414 km) of unsettled land. A fast and cheap method of transportation was needed. The completion of a transcontinental railroad became a national goal.

In 1853, Congress funded a study to determine where the railroad should be built. Citizens and politicians from every state between the East and the West lined up. They were all *vying* for the railroad to pass through their states.

President Lincoln signed the Pacific Railroad Bill in 1862. The law awarded land grants for the Union Pacific and Central Pacific Railroad companies. Each company was given land and government bonds for every mile of railroad line completed.

The Central Pacific began building from the west; the Union Pacific began building from the east. They met at Promontory Summit, Utah, on May 10, 1869.

The Last Spike was tapped into a polished laurel tie. A crowd of nearly 3,000 people was there to celebrate the "Wedding of the Rails." After the ceremony, the spike of gold and the laurel tie were withdrawn so that they would not be stolen. An iron spike and regular tie were then substituted, and east and west were finally joined.

Reading Comprehension

1. Which of these events happened next to last?
   A. Lincoln signed the Pacific Railroad Bill.
   B. Congress funded a study to determine where the railroad should be built.
   C. Leland Stanford tapped the last spike into place.
   D. The Central Pacific began building its railroad track from the west.

2. The Last Spike was made of
   A. copper.
   B. gold.
   C. titanium.
   D. zinc.

3. Why was the Last Spike removed and replaced after the ceremony?
   A. There was an issue of safety to consider.
   B. Officials were concerned that it would be stolen.
   C. The Central Pacific Railroad wanted to place the spike in a railroad museum.
   D. No one really knows why it was replaced.

4. Which of the following best defines the word *vying*?
   A. emphatically denied
   B. without care or compassion
   C. striving for
   D. preventing anyone from interfering

5. The transcontinental railroad was complete when the Last Spike was tapped into place in 1869. What advantages do you think were available after the completion of the railroad?

   _____

   _____

   _____

   _____

© Rainbow Bridge Publishing

Reading Comprehension • RB-904059

And Now . . . the Weather!

How often have you heard the question "What's the weather going to be like?" The weather is important to many Americans. For many people, checking the weather is a part of their daily routine. History tells us that it was even important to the U.S. founding fathers. George Washington kept regular notes about the weather in his diary.

President Ulysses Grant established the United States' first weather service in 1870. He assigned it to the Department of War. His justification for putting it there was that "military discipline would probably secure the greatest promptness, regularity, and accuracy in the required observations." The first *systematized*, or organized and planned, weather reports were made by officers called "observing-sergeants." The Army Signal Service maintained 22 weather stations. Each reported data by telegraph directly to Washington D.C. The service was instantly popular. Its name was changed to the Weather Bureau and then to the National Weather Service in 1967.

Early weather reports were observations of wind, air pressure, and temperature. By the middle of the twentieth century, weather was actually being predicted 48 hours in advance. Forecasts were sent to thousands of rural post offices, where they were displayed as farmers' bulletins. These updates were posted in front of the post office buildings.

Signal flags later replaced the bulletins. The flags were raised high above the post offices. Each flag had a different symbol; for example, the cold-wave flag was a large white flag with a black square in the center. Although the forecasts were not always correct, they were helpful to Americans in planning their daily lives.

Weather forecasts are more useful now than ever before. A better understanding of how the atmosphere works and developments in radar, satellite, and computing technology allow forecasters to predict the weather with increasing accuracy. Reliable short-range (12 hours–3 days) and medium-range (3–7 days) are now available for anyone who wonders, "What's the weather going to be like?"

Reading Comprehension

1. Why was the first systematized weather service placed under the Department of War?
   A. Weather reports were vital to the military.
   B. It was believed that military discipline would make weather observations more accurate.
   C. The military had more sophisticated instruments to measure the weather.
   D. Civilians did not have knowledge about the weather.

2. Which of the following elements was not included in early observations of the weather?
   A. wind speed
   B. air pressure
   C. temperature
   D. humidity

3. Which of the following best defines the word *systematized*?
   A. arranged alphabetically
   B. arranged chronologically
   C. arranged according to a defined plan
   D. arranged haphazardly

4. Which of these inventions made reporting the work of the first weather service possible?
   A. telephone
   B. telegraph
   C. radio
   D. television

5. Weather reports are an important part of the daily lives of many Americans. Are they important to you? Is there a specific part of your day during which you read, listen to, or watch a weather forecast?

   _____

   _____

   _____

© Rainbow Bridge Publishing

Reading Comprehension • RB-904059

Exxon Valdez

Early on March 24, 1989, the 987-foot-long (300.84 m) oil tanker *Exxon Valdez* slammed into Bligh Reef. Eight of the 11 cargo tanks were damaged. Nearly 11 million gallons of crude oil spilled into Prince William Sound, Alaska.

No human lives were lost in the accident, but the losses to fisheries and wildlife were huge. The livelihoods of people involved in the fishing and tourism industries were also impacted. An estimate of 250,000 seabirds and nearly 3,000 sea otters died. Hundreds of harbor seals and bald eagles were also killed. The oil spill destroyed billions of salmon eggs and herring eggs.

What actually happened remains a mystery. The captain of the *Exxon Valdez*, Joseph Hazlewood, was in his quarters at the time. However, the ship was his responsibility. Hazlewood had been seen drinking in a local bar earlier in the evening. He was charged with operating a vessel under the influence. However, an Alaskan jury declared him "not guilty."

Efforts to contain the huge spill were unsuccessful. The contamination spread as far as 460 miles (740 km). Nearly 1,300 miles (1,818 km) of *pristine* coastline were affected. In 1991, Exxon agreed to pay a penalty of $100 million. The company also said it would spend $1 billion over a 10-year period for the cost of the cleanup. The cleanup effort lasted four summers and then came to a halt. Various techniques were tried, but high-pressure cold water seemed to work the best. Not all of the affected areas were cleaned up, and weathered oil remains trapped beneath rocks and in the subsurface of some beaches.

Exxon claims to have spent about $2.1 billion on the cleanup effort. Some of the species that were nearly destroyed have recovered. Others are still recovering, and some are not recovering at all. Since the time of the accident, significant improvements have been made in the prevention of, and the plans for, responding to future oil spills. Hopefully, such a tragedy will never happen again!

Reading Comprehension

1. Which of these statements is true?
   A. The captain was found guilty of operating a vessel under the influence of alcohol.
   B. The *Exxon Valdez* ruptured when it struck an iceberg.
   C. Not all of the wildlife species have recovered from the tragedy.
   D. Exxon was held blameless by the courts for the tragic disaster.

2. Which of the following best defines the word *pristine*?
   A. unconnected   B. uncovered
   C. unspoiled   D. undulated

3. After four summers of efforts to clean up the huge oil spill,
   A. all of the affected species have recovered.
   B. the 1,300 miles of affected coastline were restored to their pristine condition.
   C. some beaches still have oil trapped beneath rocks and in the subsurface.
   D. efforts were intensified and many new cleanup techniques were tested.

4. Which of the following industries do you think was least impacted by the *Exxon Valdez* oil spill?
   A. commercial fishing   B. sport fishing
   C. tourism   D. lumbering

5. Fifteen years after the incident, opinions about the success of Exxon's cleanup of the disaster still remain mixed. Some think that Exxon did a good job, while others feel that the company did not do nearly enough. What is your opinion? Justify your conclusions.

_____

_____

_____

_____

© Rainbow Bridge Publishing

Affirmed by a Nose

As of 2006, only 11 horses have won the elusive Triple Crown of horse racing. Of the 11 horses, three won during the 1970s. Only three-year-old horses are eligible to run in Triple Crown races. The first jewel in the Triple Crown is the Kentucky Derby. It is held on the first Saturday in May at Churchill Downs racetrack in Louisville, Kentucky. The race's distance is 1¼ miles (2.01 km).

In 1978, two horses stood out as real possibilities to win the Triple Crown. Affirmed was a small horse in comparison to other champions, standing only 15.3 *hands high*. Alydar was a much larger horse. When they were two-year-olds, the two faced each other six times, with Affirmed winning four times and Alydar winning twice.

In the Derby, Alydar started from the back of the field, but was well-known for his late charges. This time he waited too long to mount his charge, and Affirmed won the first leg of the Triple Crown.

The Preakness is the second leg of the Triple Crown. It is run at Pimlico racetrack outside of Baltimore, Maryland. The distance of the Preakness is the shortest of the Triple Crown races at 1³⁄₁₆ miles (1.91 km). The strategy of Alydar's trainer changed after the Derby. This time, he wanted his horse to remain closer to the front-runners. The strategy almost worked, as Alydar closed on the lead, and Affirmed won only by a neck.

The Triple Crown's final leg is the Belmont Stakes, a race of 1½ miles (2.41 km). This race should have favored the bigger, longer-striding Alydar. However, Affirmed held on to win by a nose and, thus, became a Triple Crown champion.

Reading Comprehension

1. Which of these is the shortest racing distance in the Triple Crown?
   A. the Belmont Stakes
   B. the Kentucky Derby
   C. the Preakness
   D. none of the above

2. Which of the following best defines the phrase *hands high*?
   A. the crowd's reaction to the winning horse
   B. a measurement that describes the margin of victory in a horse race
   C. a measurement used in describing the height of a horse
   D. the position of the starter in a horse race

3. Which of these statements is false?
   A. As of 2006, only 11 horses have been Triple Crown champions.
   B. Only two-year-old horses are allowed to run in Triple Crown races.
   C. The first of the Triple Crown races is always the Kentucky Derby.
   D. Affirmed was smaller than his rival, Alydar.

4. Which of these events happened second?
   A. Affirmed defeated Alydar by a nose in the Belmont Stakes.
   B. Affirmed won the 1978 Kentucky Derby.
   C. As a two-year-old, Affirmed won four of six races against Alydar.
   D. Affirmed won the Preakness by a neck.

5. Owners spend thousands of dollars to buy, breed, and train thoroughbred horses. Why do you think there have been only 11 Triple Crown winners through the years?

   _____

   _____

   _____

   _____

© Rainbow Bridge Publishing

The First Lady of Song

When 16-year-old Ella Fitzgerald stepped onto the stage to perform at Harlem's Apollo Theater in 1934, she had no idea that her life was about to change. Her childhood had been rough. After the death of her parents, Fitzgerald had been placed in a boarding school. Unfortunately, the faculty at the school mistreated her, so she ran away. Homeless and orphaned, Fitzgerald was struggling to survive on the streets of New York City when she won a contest to perform during an amateur night at the Apollo. She had originally planned to dance, but at the last second, she decided to sing her mother's favorite song instead. Her performance earned her recognition from several well-known musicians. Ella Fitzgerald went on to became a *renowned* jazz singer.

During a musical career that spanned six decades, Fitzgerald released more than 200 albums. She won 13 Grammy Awards, the last of which she received in 1990. She worked with some of the greatest American singers of the twentieth century, including Frank Sinatra, Louis Armstrong, Count Basie, and Dizzy Gillespie. Her talent and charisma appealed to a wide range of listeners around the world. The worldwide admiration of Ella Fitzgerald helped make jazz a more popular genre.

Until the Civil Rights Movement of the 1960s, the United States denied African American citizens the same treatment that white citizens received. Fitzgerald's manager and her band refused to perform at places where discrimination was practiced. They also decided not to perform unless they were paid the same amount as white singers and musicians. Ella's fight for equality received support from numerous celebrity admirers, including Marilyn Monroe. Fitzgerald never took her good fortune for granted. She gave money to charities and organizations that were devoted caring for disadvantaged children. For her many civic contributions, in 1992 President George Bush awarded her the Presidential Medal of Honor, one of the highest honors available to civilians.

In 1991, Fitzgerald gave her final performance in New York's Carnegie Hall. Although Ella Fitzgerald died in 1996, the American "First Lady of Song" continues to live in the hearts and ears of music lovers worldwide.

© Rainbow Bridge Publishing *Reading Comprehension* • RB-904059

Reading Comprehension

1. Which of the following best defines the word *renowned*?
   A. wealthy
   B. talented
   C. famous
   D. underappreciated

2. Number the following events in the order that they happened.

   _____ Fitzgerald won a contest to perform during amateur night at the Apollo Theater in New York City.

   _____ Fitzgerald was orphaned and placed in a boarding school.

   _____ Fitzgerald received the Presidential Medal of Honor.

   _____ Fitzgerald gave her final performance.

   _____ Fitzgerald received her final Grammy Award.

3. How did Fitzgerald help make jazz a more popular musical genre?
   A. She advertised on television, which helped her music become more popular.
   B. Fitzgerald's talent and charisma appealed to listeners around the world.
   C. She often sang duets with unknown musicians so that they could also become famous.
   D. None of the above.

4. Why do you think Ella Fitzgerald is called the "First Lady of Song"?

   _____

   _____

   _____

   _____

© Rainbow Bridge Publishing

Reading Comprehension · RB-904059

The Great Grocery Debate

Most people trust that the food that they buy at the grocery store is safe. The U.S. Food and Drug Administration regulates foods to make sure that they are not harmful. But, some people argue that we buy and eat unsafe foods every day. They think that stores should stop selling genetically modified (GM) foods.

Genetic modification is a controversial topic. Basically, it is the process in which scientists change very specific DNA sequences within the cells of plants that are used in foods. This change causes a difference in the protein production of the food. Small differences in proteins can cause large variances within the food. For example, a tomato can be genetically modified so that it will not spoil as quickly.

Opponents of GM foods argue that scientists do not understand protein production well enough to change it in foods. Creating different proteins is a very delicate and complex procedure and involves understanding the roles of various genes. These opponents argue that eating GM foods may cause side effects that are not yet known.

Supporters of GM foods say that there is no difference in safety when the DNA of foods is changed. They compare it to crossbreeding plants in order to create new breeds of fruits or vegetables. They claim that creating strains of plants that naturally create pesticides or larger, longer-lasting fruits and vegetables will help feed the world's growing population. They also note that there have been no health problems attributed to GM foods, even though GM corn, soybeans, and tomatoes have been sold in grocery stores for years.

Reading Comprehension • RB-904059

Reading Comprehension

1. Which of the following best defines the main idea of this reading?
   A. Many foods commonly sold in grocery stores are not safe.
   B. As the world's population continues to grow, farmers cannot produce enough tomatoes to meet the rising demand.
   C. The genetic modification of food is a controversial topic, and its benefits and drawbacks are not yet fully known.
   D. Genetic modification creates new breeds of fruits and vegetables.

2. Why do some people oppose the sale of genetically modified foods?

   _____

   _____

   _____

3. Name one benefit of genetically modified foods.

   _____

   _____

4. Do you think genetically modified foods should be sold in grocery stores? Explain your reasoning.

   _____

   _____

   _____

   _____

   _____

   _____

   _____

© Rainbow Bridge Publishing

About to Blow?

Three elements must come together for geysers to occur: an abundant supply of water, an intense source of heat, and unique plumbing. Water is common in nature, and heat can come from volcanic activity. It is the plumbing that is particularly critical. For water to be thrown into the air, geyser plumbing must be both water- and pressure-tight.

This proper mix is one of the things that makes Yellowstone National Park so unique. Yellowstone National Park is located on top of a collapsed supervolcano, and more than half of the world's geysers are located there. Recent concern has surfaced about a huge bulge on the floor of Yellowstone Lake. Some scientists claim that the region is "geology in the making" and think that an explosion is imminent. They are urging engineers to drill the ground and create holes to channel the steam that is creating the bulge. They claim that not doing so would risk a disastrous explosion.

Other geologists who have studied Yellowstone do not share the same concern. They say that drilling would not do any good because the magma chamber that lies beneath Yellowstone National Park is too big and too far underground to vent effectively. They do see the bulge under Yellowstone Lake as a possible sign of future activity, but some geologists say the bulge may have been there for millennia. It was revealed by new digital technology that allows geologists to see much deeper into the floor of the lake.

Bob Smith, a geophysics expert who has studied the "living *caldera*" of Yellowstone for decades, finds no indication in the park's seismic activity that an explosion will occur in the near future.

© Rainbow Bridge Publishing

Reading Comprehension • RB-904059

Reading Comprehension

1. Which of the following is not a necessary ingredient of geyser activity?
   A. water
   B. air
   C. heat
   D. pressure-tight plumbing

2. Which of the following best explains why more than half of the world's geysers are located in Yellowstone National Park?
   A. Yellowstone was the first national park in the United States.
   B. Yellowstone National Park is located on a collapsed supervolcano.
   C. Old Faithful is the world's most spectacular geyser.
   D. Geysers are usually found in the western United States.

3. Which of the following best defines the word *caldera*?
   A. a large pot used for cooking
   B. volcanic ash accumulated from nearby eruptions
   C. a huge bulge in an underground lake
   D. a volcanic crater formed by the collapse of a volcano

4. Which of the following is not a reason why some geologists are unconcerned about an explosion occurring at Yellowstone National Park?
   A. The bulge under Yellowstone Lake could have been there for a long time.
   B. Digital technology has allowed geologists to see more deeply into the bottom of the lake than ever before.
   C. The seismic activity at Yellowstone does not indicate that an explosion will occur.
   D. Recent changes in the geyser basin indicate that a huge explosion is about to happen.

5. Do you think that news of the discovery of the bulging activity on the floor of Yellowstone Lake will have any effect on the number of visitors to Yellowstone Park?

   _____

   _____

   _____

© Rainbow Bridge Publishing

Why Sunsets Are Beautiful

Most of us have enjoyed the beautiful red and orange colors of a sunset. Although colorful sunsets can be seen anywhere, certain parts of the world (for example, in deserts or the tropics) are especially well-known for their magnificent sunsets. Clean air is the main ingredient in a brilliant sunset.

The color that we see in the sky is the result of the scattering, *refraction*, and diffraction of sunlight by particles—such as air molecules—in the atmosphere. If there were no particles in the atmosphere, the sunlight would simply travel straight down to Earth, and the sky would be black.

Sunlight is composed of a mixture of colors (red, orange, yellow, green, blue, indigo, and violet). Each color in this spectrum has a different wavelength. Red and orange have the longest wavelengths. Blue, indigo, and violet have the shortest.

When sunlight enters Earth's atmosphere, air molecules bend and scatter the colors. The air molecules first scatter the colors that have the shortest wavelengths. When the sun is high, the light's pathway to Earth is shorter, so violet, indigo, blue, and a little green are scattered where we can see them. The result is a blue sky. When the sun is low in the sky, at either sunrise or sunset, the path through the atmosphere is longer. A longer trip gives the blue color so much room to scatter that we can no longer see it. Only the red, yellow, and orange reach our eyes.

The farther light travels through the atmosphere, the redder it appears. In the United States, at the same moment a beam of sunlight is producing a red sunset over the Appalachians, it is also making the sky a deep blue in the West.

Reading Comprehension • RB-904059

Reading Comprehension

1. Which of the following best explains why sunsets are especially beautiful in deserts and the tropics?
   A. Deserts and the tropics typically have cleaner air.
   B. Deserts and the tropics have longer light rays.
   C. Deserts and the tropics have more clouds.
   D. Deserts and the tropics have longer days.

2. Which of the following statements is false?
   A. The farther light travels through the atmosphere, the redder it appears.
   B. The sky would be black if sunlight traveled straight down to Earth.
   C. The sky is blue because the light waves near the blue end of the spectrum have the greatest distance to travel.
   D. Light rays bend and scatter when they encounter air molecules in the atmosphere.

3. Which of the following best defines the word *refraction*?
   A. deflection from a straight path
   B. following an intended course
   C. contributing to mirrored reflection
   D. reversing directions

4. The last sentence in the reading could best be characterized as which of the following?
   A. authorization to close
   B. dramatic conclusion
   C. summarizing example
   D. punctuating footnote

5. Explain why we sometimes see red sunsets.

   _____

   _____

   _____

   _____

© Rainbow Bridge Publishing
Reading Comprehension · RB-904059

Stuffed Love

A teddy bear is often a child's first toy. You may have had one of your own. There are many different versions of the story of how the teddy bear got its name, but many of them involve a man who was the president of the United States.

One story begins when President Theodore "Teddy" Roosevelt traveled to Mississippi in 1902 to settle a border dispute between Mississippi and Louisiana. While he was there, he went on a hunting trip. He and his hunting party hiked and climbed for three days without spotting any animals. Finally, members of the party found a bear. The bear was wounded in a fight with the group's hunting dogs. Some members of the hunting party tied the injured bear to a tree for President Roosevelt to shoot. However, Roosevelt refused to harm the bear for sport.

The next day, political cartoonist Clifford Berryman drew a cartoon that showed Roosevelt refusing to hurt the bear. His caption was "Drawing the Line in Mississippi." It was a *dual reference* to the border dispute and the hunting incident. After seeing the cartoon, a New York shopkeeper had an idea. He asked his wife to make two stuffed bears to display in his shop's window. They were an instant hit with the public. The shopkeeper decided to capitalize on the connection between his plush bears and President Roosevelt. He asked the president for permission to call his bears "Teddy bears." Roosevelt agreed, and the teddy bear was born.

Another version of the story begins in Germany. Richard Steiff, nephew of the founder of the Steiff Company, had seen a troupe of performing bears. He had an idea for a new toy bear that stood on two feet rather than all four. He showed his first bear at the Leipzig Toy Fair in 1903. An American toy distributor immediately ordered 3,000 bears.

These two stories connect with the marriage of Teddy Roosevelt's daughter. A member of the decorating committee saw one of the Steiff bears in a New York toy store. She bought several to use as table decorations for the reception. One of the guests reportedly asked the president what breed of bear the decorations represented. He could not answer, but another guest said, "They're Teddy bears, of course!"

© Rainbow Bridge Publishing

Reading Comprehension

1. Which of these events happened last?
   A. Theodore Roosevelt went on a hunting trip while he was in Mississippi.
   B. Clifford Berryman's cartoon inspired a New York shopkeeper to create a plush stuffed bear.
   C. Theodore Roosevelt's daughter used several teddy bears as table decorations for her wedding reception.
   D. Richard Steiff showed a toy bear that stood on its two hind legs at the Leipzig Toy Fair.

2. Which of the following best defines the phrase *dual reference*?
   A. a double-edged sword
   B. a subject with two possible varying interpretations
   C. the other side of the coin, which is "tails"
   D. none of the above

3. Which of the following would be another good title for this reading?
   A. Bears across America
   B. Everybody Loves Teddy!
   C. Roosevelt Saves the Day!
   D. Defenseless Bear in Mississippi

4. Which of the following events was probably least responsible for the teddy bear we know today?
   A. President Roosevelt's hunting trip in Mississippi
   B. Clifford Berryman's political cartoon
   C. the shopkeeper's display of two stuffed bears
   D. President Roosevelt's determination to solve the border dispute between Mississippi and Louisiana

5. Do you think we would still have plush stuffed bears if the events in the reading had never happened? Explain your answer.

   _____

   _____

   _____

   _____

© Rainbow Bridge Publishing   *Reading Comprehension* • RB-904059

Mystery of the *Maine*

Relations between the United States and Spain were not very good in 1898. On February 15, a battleship called the USS *Maine* blew up and sank in the harbor at Havana, Cuba. More than 260 Americans were killed. Many Americans thought that Spanish *saboteurs* had set an underwater mine that caused the explosion.

Witnesses and survivors had different versions of what happened. Some said that they heard two explosions. It was discovered that the magazine —which is a storage place for arms, ammunition, and explosives—had exploded. Questions were raised about what caused the first explosion. Did the first explosion come from outside the ship, causing the magazine to explode? Or, did something on the ship ignite the magazine?

Other witnesses said that there was only one explosion. If they are right, then what on the ship caused the magazine to explode? A theory supporting the two-explosion version was that rebels from Cuba had caused the explosion. The rebels were aware of the bad feelings between the United States and Spain. They would have been willing to cause trouble between the nations to bring an end to Spanish rule in Cuba.

The United States government issued an ultimatum to the Spanish government to end its occupation of Cuba. When Spanish officials refused, Congress and President William McKinley declared war on Spain. The war did not last long, because the United States forced an early surrender.

More than 100 years after the explosion of the *Maine*, the cause of the explosion is still unknown. Many questions remain. If an attack from outside the ship caused the magazine to explode, why didn't witnesses see a splash in the water? Why were there no dead fish in the water if there was an external explosion?

With the mystery still unsolved, the question of what really happened to the USS *Maine* may never be answered.

© Rainbow Bridge Publishing

Reading Comprehension

1. Which of these statements is false?
   A. Some witnesses said that they heard a single explosion.
   B. The explosion caused more than 260 Americans to lose their lives.
   C. The explosion of the USS *Maine* is the spark that ignited the war with Spain.
   D. Solving the mystery of the destruction of the USS *Maine* was a proud moment for the CIA.

2. Which of the following best defines the word *saboteurs*?
   A. people who secretly destroy the property or lives of others
   B. spies who use advanced technology to gather information
   C. soldiers who board and loot battleships
   D. sailors who abandon their ship to avoid enemy capture

3. Those who believe in the single-explosion theory must reach the following conclusion:
   A. An outside force must have attacked the ship.
   B. The explosion of the magazine must have been triggered by something on the ship.
   C. Cuban rebels caused the explosion.
   D. none of the above

4. Which best explains the motive of Cuban rebels to cause the explosion?
   A. They were mean-spirited.
   B. They were hoping that the United States would bring an end to Spanish rule in Cuba.
   C. They wanted to return to their native country, Spain.
   D. The United States refused to surrender the *Maine* to the rebels.

5. Do you think that the mystery of the USS *Maine* will ever be solved? Explain your answer.

   _____

   _____

   _____

© Rainbow Bridge Publishing   *Reading Comprehension* • RB-904059

America's Aging Population

The number of American seniors is growing more quickly than any other segment of the population. Better eating habits, more exercise, and advances in medical care are helping Americans live longer and heathier lives.

This is, of course, good news. However, an aging population has needs that are not being met. One of these needs is public transportation. Traveling by car should not be a senior citizen's only option. There is a growing need for the benefits that public transportation can provide older Americans.

America's older citizens require increased mobility. With better public transportation, seniors would have more options when choosing where to live. They would also have more choices when deciding how and where they would like to travel. Better public transportation could help America's senior citizens lead more active lives.

According to the U.S. Census Bureau, more than 35 million Americans were 65 years old or older in the year 2000. Because there was a baby boom—an increase in births—between 1946 and 1964, the senior population in America will grow much faster than the rest of the population. Many older people already live in suburban locations that lack transit options, and as the *baby boomers* age, the number of older citizens who live in these areas will continue to increase.

Isolation is a growing problem for elderly Americans. Not only does it affect their ability to take care of their basic needs, it also affects their ability to make contributions to their neighborhoods and society as a whole. This isolation is felt most by those who are over the age of 85 and who have medical conditions that prevent them from driving.

Many people think that the answer to solving this problem of mobility for an aging population is simple. They believe that public transportation systems must be upgraded and expanded so that seniors have the resources available to meet their transportation needs.

Reading Comprehension

1. What is the main theme of this reading?
   A. why Americans are living longer
   B. facing growing poverty among senior citizens
   C. facing senior-citizen transportation problems
   D. tackling the issue of housing for senior citizens

2. Which of the following is not a benefit of public transportation for the elderly?
   A. It gives them greater mobility.
   B. They have greater access to varied destinations.
   C. They have greater freedom to live in a variety of places.
   D. It allows them to travel with their unleashed pets.

3. Which of the following best defines the phrase *baby boomer*?
   A. a child with parents who are no longer living
   B. a person born between 1946 and 1964
   C. a child who has retired parents
   D. a child who weighed more than 8.5 pounds (3.86 kg) at birth

4. Why is America's population of senior citizens increasing in number?
   A. They are more health conscious about the foods that they eat and are getting more exercise.
   B. There was a baby boom between 1946 and 1964.
   C. There have been many advances in medicine that contribute to longer lives.
   D. all of the above

5. Why is isolation becoming a growing problem among elderly people, especially those over the age of 85?

   _____

   _____

   _____

   _____

© Rainbow Bridge Publishing

Reading Comprehension • RB-904059

All Charged Up!

The electric eel is not really an eel. Electric eels are actually members of a group of electrical fish. All of their vital organs are located in the *anterior* one-fifth of their bodies. Most of an eel's length consists of its long, electricity-producing tail. Electric eels can grow to be quite large, up to eight feet (2.4 m) in length and 60 pounds (27.2 kg) in weight. The eel has an elongated fin which extends from the tip of its tail almost to its throat, but it does not have a dorsal fin. Electric eels also do not have teeth.

Although electric eels are capable of producing powerful shocks, they are not aggressive. They use their electrical abilities to protect themselves from predators and to immobilize their prey. Electric eels also use weaker electrical signals to navigate and to communicate with each other in the muddy rivers where they live.

Just how strong can an eel's electrical shock be? The eel is capable of producing an electrical discharge of up to 600 volts. That is more than enough to kill a small fish for food. It is also enough to deal with its potential predators. A touch from the eel's tail can effectively disable a human. Its tail contains specialized electric organs. These organs consist of thousands of cells called electroplaques. The eel's electrical system is similar to a row of connected batteries. After the eel delivers a strong shock, its electric organ needs time to recharge.

Electric eels are popular in public aquariums but, if released into the wild outside of their South American habitat, could create quite a hazard. Due to their large size and habit of giving shocks, even when treated gently, electric eels are best left to professional keepers.

Reading Comprehension

1. Which of these statements is false?
   A. The electric eel can produce a shock of up to 600 volts.
   B. The shock from an electric eel will kill most human beings.
   C. Electric eels can grow up to 8 feet (2.4 m) in length.
   D. Electric eels are typically not very aggressive.

2. Which of the following best defines the word *anterior*?
   A. near the back
   B. near the front
   C. at an angled position
   D. away from the center

3. The electrical system within the electric eel is much like that of
   A. a set of four AA batteries in a radio.
   B. a set of size C batteries arranged in a flashlight.
   C. a row of connected batteries.
   D. a turbine in an electricity-producing plant.

4. Electric eels use their electricity for
   A. navigation.
   B. communication.
   C. defense against predators.
   D. all of the above

5. What do you think would happen if you encountered an electric eel while you were swimming?

   _____

   _____

   _____

   _____

   _____

   _____

© Rainbow Bridge Publishing

The Big Dance

The NCAA Men's Basketball Championship is one of the top attractions in college sports. Often called "March Madness" or "The Big Dance," the hype that accompanies this tournament can make basketball fans out of people who are not usually interested in the sport.

The first NCAA basketball tournament was played in 1939 with only 8 teams. In 1951, the field was expanded to 16 teams. Over the years, the number of teams allowed to participate in the tournament increased steadily. In 1985, 64 teams participated. In 2001, the addition of a play-in game between the two lowest-ranked teams raised the number of teams to 65.

The four teams that reach the semifinal round have always been called the "Final Four." A team must string together four wins to reach the Final Four. Winning the national championship requires another two wins.

There are several ways that teams can qualify to play in the NCAA tournament. Some teams are chosen to play in the tournament by a selection committee. This committee studies the records and statistics of each team's season. Both a team's overall record and the difficulty of its schedule are factored into the committee's final decision. Conference tournaments held at the end of the regular season also qualify additional teams.

Late on the Sunday afternoon of the week prior to the tournament, the committee announces the 65 teams that will be playing in the tournament. It also ranks the teams and assigns where each will play. There are four regional tournaments with 16 teams in each. The winners of the four regional tournaments then meet for the final showdown and the national championship.

Reading Comprehension

1. How many games must a team consecutively win to be declared the national champion?
   A. seven
   B. five
   C. six
   D. four

2. Which happens first in the sequence of events leading up to the national championship?
   A. Teams are chosen by the selection committee.
   B. Major conferences hold their own post-season tournaments.
   C. The Final Four gather for the national championship.
   D. The four regional tournaments are played.

3. Which of the following statements is false?
   A. The first tournament was played in 1939.
   B. The semifinals are played between six teams.
   C. There are four regional tournaments.
   D. Sixty-five teams compete in the tournament.

4. Which of the following statements is true?
   A. The play-in game began in 1951.
   B. There are eight regional tournaments with eight teams in each.
   C. In 2001, the number of teams competing in the tournament rose to 65.
   D. To qualify for the tournament, a team must win at least 20 games.

5. Why do you think so many people—even those who don't usually follow sports—become emotionally invested in championship games like the NCAA Men's Basketball Championship or the Super Bowl?

_____

_____

_____

_____

The Blarney Stone

The Blarney Stone is located in Blarney Castle, which is in the village of Blarney in southwestern Ireland. The original castle was built from wood in the tenth century. It was rebuilt with stone around 1210. The castle was later demolished, and the present three-story structure was constructed in 1446 by Cormac Laidhir McCarthy, King of Munster.

The famous Blarney Stone is located high in the battlements of the castle. The stone is believed to be half of the Stone of Scone, which originally belonged to Scotland. Scottish kings were crowned over the stone because it supposedly has magical powers.

Just how the Blarney Stone may have gotten its magical powers is unclear. One legend says that an old woman cast a spell on the stone to reward a king who had saved her from drowning. Kissing the stone while under the spell gave the king the ability to speak convincingly. Today, we call it the "gift of gab."

The word *blarney* means "to placate with soft talk or to deceive without offending." Some say that the definition comes from the many unfulfilled promises of Cormac McCarthy. He had promised to give his castle to the Crown. He delayed doing so with soft words, which Queen Elizabeth I described as "blarney talk." Others say that the definition came from a king who once lived in the castle. He had the ability to remain in the middle of an argument without taking sides.

Thousands of tourists visit the castle every year. Those who kiss the Blarney Stone do so with great difficulty. They have to lie on their backs and bend backward and down, holding on to iron bars for support.

Reading Comprehension • RB-904059

Reading Comprehension

1. What is the setting for this reading?
   A. Scotland
   B. London
   C. Ireland
   D. Wales

2. Which of the following best defines the word *blarney*?
   A. understandable conversation   B. keeping thoughts inside
   C. skillful flattery   D. nonstop chattering

3. Which of the following would be the most logical conclusion from reading this legend?
   A. Most legends really do have some basis of truth.
   B. The Blarney Stone does not exist.
   C. The word *blarney* was coined from the legend of the Blarney Stone.
   D. Kissing the Blarney Stone is a custom with no value.

4. Which of these statements is false?
   A. The present structure of Blarney Castle was built in 1446.
   B. The legend of Cormac McCarthy claims that he avoided surrendering ownership of his castle by speaking with soft words.
   C. The Blarney Stone is located on the ground floor of Blarney Castle.
   D. Kissing the Blarney Stone is not an easy task.

5. If you could kiss the Blarney Stone, would you? Explain why or why not.

   _____

   _____

   _____

   _____

   _____

   _____

© Rainbow Bridge Publishing   *Reading Comprehension* • RB-904059

Hay-Fever Season

Many people know what pollen allergy is, but not everyone realizes that hay fever and pollen allergy are the same thing. In 1819, Dr. John Bostock first described the *symptoms* of hay fever to the Royal Medical Society in London, England. He spent several years studying its causes. He concluded that the cause was freshly cut hay, so he gave the condition its common name—hay fever. It was not until 1873 that another researcher, Dr. Charles Blackley, published his studies on this illness. His work showed that hay fever was caused by grass pollens. Today, hay fever is often referred to as "seasonal allergies."

Sometimes, allergies are an inherited trait. However, allergies can affect anybody, at any age. During the time of year when trees, grasses, plants, and weeds are pollinating, everyone in the area is exposed. People with allergies may become sensitive to one or more of the pollens. In addition to pollen, other airborne allergens such as dust, pet dander, mold, and fungus spores can also cause allergic reactions.

People who suffer from hay fever are most affected by pollens that become airborne. Bees and other insects transport heavier pollens between plants. Because these heavy pollens never become airborne, a person must come into contact with the plant to be affected by the pollen.

The immune system of a person with allergies mistakes pollen as a harmful substance. It also produces an antibody to fight the pollen. Some people experience cold-like symptoms when this occurs. Sneezing is the most common symptom of hay fever. A stuffy and watery nose is another sign. Others include redness, swelling, and itching of the eyes and itching of the nose and throat. These symptoms are the result of the antibodies trying to remove the pollen from the body.

The best way to control hay fever is to avoid pollen and other triggers. That is sometimes impossible. Air purification systems that work to eliminate pollen and other allergens from the air can help prevent allergic reactions. Antihistamines and decongestants can also be useful in reducing some of the symptoms that accompany hay fever.

Reading Comprehension

1. Which of the following is not a symptom of hay fever?
   A. sneezing
   B. swollen, itchy eyes
   C. hives
   D. watery nose

2. Which of the following is the most common cause of hay fever?
   A. airborne pollens
   B. bee stings
   C. direct contact with plants
   D. none of the above

3. Which of the following best defines the word *symptoms*?
   A. evidence of mistreatment
   B. things that indicate the presence of bodily disorder
   C. where pollen viruses live
   D. airborne disturbances in the atmosphere

4. Which of the following best explains why some people are allergic to certain pollens?
   A. the lifestyle that a person leads
   B. the time of the year
   C. a family trait that was inherited
   D. close contact with an infected person

5. Describe effective ways that an allergy sufferer can avoid some of the misery that is associated with hay fever.

   _____

   _____

   _____

   _____

   _____

   _____

© Rainbow Bridge Publishing

Garlic's Time

Garlic, a common seasoning found in many different types of food, has a long medical and mythical history. References to garlic are found in Chinese texts that are dated as far back as 3000 BC. The physician Hippocrates used garlic in ancient Greece to treat infections and intestinal disorders. In many parts of the ancient world, garlic was also thought to ward off unfriendly spirits, treat wounds, and protect against disease.

Roman soldiers believed that garlic brought them courage and stamina. They took it with them when they went into battle. Egyptians fed garlic to their servants when they built pyramids. They thought that it gave the workers strength. They also believed that garlic had magical and medicinal powers. In the Middle Ages, people thought that garlic prevented the plague.

People have praised the virtues of garlic for centuries. Although garlic's popularity began to *wane* in the early years of the twentieth century, its reputation has been restored in recent years. It is now a valuable cash crop in the state of California. Nearly a half-billion pounds of garlic are produced there each year. The city of Gilroy, California, considers itself the garlic capital of the world. Each year, the city hosts the Gilroy Garlic Festival in honor of the crop.

Some doctors are studying garlic's effects as a defense against some forms of cancer. Others are exploring its possibilities for treating arthritis. Garlic has also received praise for its ability to lower high blood pressure. More recently, it has been linked to reducing high levels of cholesterol. Although some of the medicinal benefits of garlic have yet to be proven, it is certain that many people enjoy the flavor that it adds to food.

© Rainbow Bridge Publishing

Reading Comprehension • RB-904059

Reading Comprehension

1. Which of these statements is a fact?
   A. Garlic makes food taste great.
   B. Garlic prevents cancer.
   C. Garlic can cure arthritis.
   D. Garlic was used for medicinal purposes in ancient times.

2. Which of the following best identifies the time setting of this reading?
   A. 4,000 years ago
   B. 2,000 years ago
   C. today
   D. ancient history to the present

3. Which of the following statements is not discussed in the article?
   A. Garlic is a valuable cash crop in California.
   B. Hippocrates found several uses for garlic.
   C. Garlic is currently used as a meat substitute in certain diet plans.
   D. Garlic was thought to bring courage and stamina to Roman soldiers.

4. Which of the following best defines the word *wane*?
   A. dwindle
   B. increase
   C. become grateful
   D. pass in silence

5. Even if only a few of the claims that people have made about the uses of garlic are true, why doesn't everyone use garlic on a daily basis?

   _____

   _____

   _____

   _____

© Rainbow Bridge Publishing

Asteroids

In 1801, Giuseppe Piazzi discovered a new object in the sky. He thought it was an undiscovered comet. After further observation, he realized that it behaved more like a small planet than a comet. Piazzi named it Ceres after the Sicilian goddess of grain. Ceres remains the largest known asteroid in the sky. It measures almost 600 miles (1,000 km) in diameter. By the end of the nineteenth century, several hundred other asteroids had been identified.

Tens of thousands of asteroids have since been discovered, with thousands more found each year. Asteroids are lumps of rock and metal that orbit the sun between Mars and Jupiter. They did not form into planets because the *perturbations* of Jupiter kept them moving too fast to join together. The total mass of all of the asteroids is less than the size of Earth's moon.

Some of the asteroids move in orbits outside the zone between Mars and Jupiter. Asteroids that come relatively close to Earth are known as near-Earth asteroids (NEAs). Scientists estimate that about 1,000 of these asteroids are .6 miles (1 km) in diameter. An asteroid of this size colliding with Earth would be disastrous.

Scientists have found two sites where giant asteroids struck Earth millions of years ago. One asteroid hit Antarctica about 250 million years ago. Another asteroid struck Mexico's Yucatan Peninsula around 65 million years ago, leaving a crater 112 miles (180 km) wide and 1,000 yards (914 m) deep. One theory blames the extinction of the dinosaurs on this asteroid's collision with Earth and the climate change that resulted from its impact.

Occasionally, small asteroids strike Earth. These cause little damage. Major collisions, such as the one that may have killed the dinosaurs, occur rarely—perhaps only once every 100 million years.

Although the chance of an asteroid striking the planet anytime soon is small, scientists continue to study the orbits of asteroids in the sky. They pay particularly close attention to the asteroids whose paths are close to Earth, and have even landed a spacecraft on an NEA named Eros. Their work helps them learn about the formation of the solar system. It may even help them discover ways to avoid an asteroid disaster in the future.

Reading Comprehension • RB-904059

Reading Comprehension

1. Which of these events happened third?
   A. Giuseppe Piazzi discovered Ceres.
   B. Scientists had a spacecraft land on Eros.
   C. Lumps of orbiting rock and material failed to form into planets.
   D. Several hundred asteroids had been identified by the end of the nineteenth century.

2. Which of these statements is false?
   A. No asteroid has ever crashed into Earth.
   B. Asteroids orbit the sun between Mars and Jupiter.
   C. Asteroids are composed of rock and metal.
   D. A large asteroid colliding with Earth would cause a disaster.

3. Which of the following best defines the word *perturbations*?
   A. elliptical disturbances of motion   B. powerful radioactive heat
   C. large craters   D. sound waves

4. Where are most asteroids found?
   A. between New York and California
   B. between Mars and Jupiter
   C. between Earth and Mars
   D. between Neptune and Mercury

5. In February of 2004, a conference on protecting Earth from asteroids was held in Garden Grove, California. What are some of the topics that you think these scientists might have placed on their agenda?

   _____

   _____

   _____

   _____

© Rainbow Bridge Publishing

Totem Poles

The first explorers who saw totem poles called them "monstrous figures." Missionaries thought that the Native Americans worshipped the totem poles, and they encouraged their destruction. But, the missionaries were wrong. Even today, when people refer to the "low man on the totem pole," they do not realize that the largest figure was usually on the bottom and was the most important.

The origin of the first totem pole is uncertain. It is known that totem poles told stories about rich and important Native American families. An artist carved the pole to represent a family's traits and personal strengths and even to have hidden meanings.

Poles were carved from cedar, using handmade tools. The chisel used for carving was made from an animal horn. The *adze*, which was like an ax, had a hard stone blade. Once finished carving, the artist used animal-hair brushes to paint the poles. Some poles stood as high as 60 feet (180 m).

Native Americans celebrated important life events—such as births or marriages—with huge feasts called potlatches. One of the highlights of the party was the raising of a new totem pole. As trade expanded along the Northwest Coast, more Native American families had totem poles.

However, in 1884 the Canadian government outlawed the potlatch. Not long after, the United States followed suit. As children grew up and left the tribe, the art of carving totem poles began to die out.

Many years later, totem poles that had been bought or stolen from Native American villages began showing up in museums. People started to realize the significance of totem poles, and the art of carving them was resurrected. Old poles were restored, and new poles were created. Today, the craft is alive and well again, and totem poles can be seen around the Northwest United States and Canada.

Reading Comprehension

1. Which of these statements best explains the purpose of totem poles?
   A. They could scare away enemy tribes.
   B. They were used as centerpieces in some religions.
   C. They told of the accomplishments of the more important families.
   D. They were carved as a mystery to keep European explorers guessing.

2. One of the tools used in the carving of totem poles was a tool like an ax called a (an)
   A. chisel.
   B. maul.
   C. hammer.
   D. adze.

3. Which of the following best explains why the art of carving totem poles faded away during the 1800s?
   A. Family pride was no longer important to Native Americans.
   B. The Canadian and United States' governments took away all of the tools used to carve totem poles.
   C. There were no more stories to tell when the settlers took possession of the land.
   D. Many of the children left their tribes, and the art began to die out.

4. Which of the following locations defines the setting for this reading?
   A. Pacific Northwest of the United States and Canada
   B. Southern California
   C. Northern Alaska and Russia
   D. The desert Southwestern of the United States

5. What factors do you think were responsible for the revival of the art of totem poles during the 1960s and 1970s?

   _____

   _____

   _____

   _____

   _____

© Rainbow Bridge Publishing

A Rare Find

One of the world's most valuable stamps was sold at an auction in 1980 for $935,000. The stamp is an 1856 British Guiana Penny Magenta. The corners have been snipped off, so the stamp is actually octagonal in shape.

During the 1800s, stamps used in British Guiana were printed in England. In 1856, the stock of stamps sold out before a new shipment arrived. The postmaster asked the publishers of a local newspaper to print some for people to use until the new stamps arrived. One-cent stamps were to be used for newspapers. Four-cent stamps were for letters. Both stamps were printed in black ink on magenta paper.

The postmaster asked postal employees to initial each stamp to prevent forgery. Several years later, a 12-year-old boy, who had a stamp collection, was foraging through some family papers. He discovered the octagonal-shaped, one-cent stamp postmarked "April 4, 1856." It bore the initials "E.D.W." He kept the stamp for several weeks and then sold it to a local stamp collector for about a dollar.

Several *philatelists* bought and sold the stamp through the years. As time passed, it became obvious that the stamp was very rare, because no other copy was ever found.

In 1970, the same stamp was sold at an auction for $280,000 to Irwin Weinberg and a group of investors. The stamp remained in their collection until 1980, when it was sold to John E. du Pont for $935,000. Currently, the Penny Magenta remains locked in a bank vault in Philadelphia, Pennsylvania.

© Rainbow Bridge Publishing

Reading Comprehension

1. Which of the following best defines the word *philatelist*?
    A. stamp maker
    B. stamp designer
    C. stamp collector
    D. stamper

2. Which statement offers the best explanation for the high cost that collectors were willing to pay for the stamp?
    A. It is printed in black ink on magenta paper.
    B. The corners are snipped off to give it a unique shape.
    C. No similar stamps have ever been discovered.
    D. The stamp has three initials written on it.

3. How was the stamp first discovered?
    A. The local postmaster secretly kept one in his drawer.
    B. It was discovered by a stamp collector on the Internet.
    C. The famous wrestler John du Pont found it in his garage.
    D. A boy found it in some family papers.

4. What was the original value of the British Guiana Penny Magenta stamp?
    A. one dollar
    B. one penny
    C. four cents
    D. a nickel

5. What factors determine the value of a stamp?

    _____

    _____

    _____

    _____

    _____

© Rainbow Bridge Publishing

The Great Wall

Not only is the Great Wall of China the longest structure ever built, it was also constructed entirely by hand. The first section of the wall was built in the central part of the country during the seventh century. Small kingdoms in the Chu period of China's history built walls to mark their territories and keep out invaders. It was during the Qin dynasty (221–206 BC) that the emperor began to build and connect the many walls into a single wall. Eventually, the Great Wall extended to a distance of about 4,500 miles (7,240 km).

The sections of the wall were built from a variety of materials. Portions of the wall were constructed of crudely fashioned bricks. Some sections were made of stones that were local to the area. In the east, the wall has a foundation of granite blocks and sides of stone or brick. Where stone was scarce, workers used hardened earth, sand, or mud. In some areas, no mortar was used to hold the stones together.

The wall also varies in height and width. One of the highest sections is 35 feet (11 m) tall. It is 25 feet (7.6 m) wide at the base. There are also towers along many parts of the wall, which served as lookout stations. Some sections of the wall were "double-layered" to provide even more protection.

The Great Wall served as more than just protection from attacks from the north. It also provided a physical boundary between China and northern lands. Winding its way through mountainous regions and bordering some desert areas, the wall was a well-fortified highway for traveling merchants and for moving troops.

The Great Wall has been *renovated* many times throughout the ages. The most ambitious of these projects was started during the Ming dynasty in 1368. This major part of the wall is the most modern section and attracts many visitors today. Although parts of the wall have disappeared completely, there are sections of the wall that are in remarkably good condition. Now, steps are being taken to protect the wall from further destruction and decay.

© Rainbow Bridge Publishing *Reading Comprehension* • RB-904059

Reading Comprehension

1. Which of the following best defines the word *renovated*?
   A. rebuilt
   B. revisited
   C. repaired
   D. returned

2. Which of the following best describes the location of the Great Wall of China?
   A. across northern China
   B. between China and Russia
   C. along the eastern edge of China, near the East China Sea
   D. separating China from Africa

3. Which of these statements is false?
   A. Sections of the wall were built to keep out invaders from the north.
   B. Various sections of the wall were constructed from different building materials.
   C. Lavish shops and restaurants were built along the length of the wall for troops and travelers.
   D. Sections of the wall marked territory owned by various states.

4. The Great Wall of China is the longest man-made structure on Earth, stretching for a distance of approximately
   A. 2,000 miles (3,219 km).
   B. 4,500 miles (7,242 km).
   C. 8,000 miles (12, 875 km).
   D. 10,000 miles (16,093 km).

5. While no one knows for sure what the motives for building the wall were, historians and archaeologists have speculated why they think it was built. Why do you think it was built?

   _____

   _____

   _____

   _____

© Rainbow Bridge Publishing

First, the Lightning

When Benjamin Franklin conducted his experiments with lightning, he was very fortunate that he was not badly hurt. Lightning is an extremely powerful force of nature. A single bolt of lightning is hotter than the surface of the sun. Although its formation is similar to that of a small spark of static electricity, a lightning strike releases a tremendous amount of energy.

During a storm, small particles in clouds collect either positive or negative charges of energy. The lighter, positively charged particles rise to the top of the clouds. The heavier, negatively charged particles fall to the bottom of the clouds. This separation creates a path through the air for the flow of electricity. Once the attraction between the two groups becomes too strong, the particles release their stored energy. This electrical discharge is lightning.

The thunder that follows the lightning is the sound made by the air as it is suddenly heated by the lightning strike. The lightning bolt can instantly heat the molecules of the air to a temperature that exceeds 50,000 degrees Fahrenheit (27,760 degrees Celsius). These heated molecules then expand and collide. This rapid explosion of air is the source of the sound waves that we call thunder.

Even though it seems like lightning and thunder occur at different times, this is only a trick of the senses. Light travels 186,282 miles (299,792 km) per second, but sound travels only 1,116 feet (340 m) per second. This difference in speed explains why lightning and thunder reach us at different times. The sound of thunder takes more time than the light from a lightning strike to travel the same distance.

To calculate your distance from a lightning strike, count the number of seconds between the flash of lightning and the sound of thunder. Then, divide that number by five. The result will be your approximate distance in miles from the lightning. The closer the lightning is to you, the closer the visible flash and the sound of thunder are to each other.

Reading Comprehension • RB-904059

Reading Comprehension

1. Which of the following best explains the sound of thunder?
   A. the principle of sound waves created by feet shuffling across a carpet
   B. the sudden rush of air found in a pressure-cooker atmosphere
   C. sound waves created by the release of heavily charged air particles
   D. emotionally charged particles of air running into physically charged particles of air

2. Why do we see the lightning first and hear the thunder later?
   A. No explanation was provided.
   B. The thunder has to travel a much greater distance.
   C. Light waves travel much faster than sound waves.
   D. Our sense of sight is stronger and more refined than our sense of hearing.

3. Which of these statements is true?
   A. A lightning strike can be as hot as 1,000,000°F (555,538°C).
   B. Light travels at one-fifth the speed of sound.
   C. Negatively charged particles rise to the top of a cloud.
   D. The closer the lightning is to you, the closer the flash of light and the sound of thunder are to each other.

4. The main difference between a lightning strike and static electricity is
   A. intensity.
   B. proximity.
   C. distance.
   D. response time.

5. Briefly explain how you can determine the distance that a lightning strike is from you.

   _____

   _____

   _____

   _____

© Rainbow Bridge Publishing

Reading Comprehension • RB-904059

Stitches

Humans have sewn by hand for thousands of years. The first thread was made from animal sinew. Needles were made from bones. Since those early days, many people have been involved in the process of developing a machine that could do the same thing more quickly and with greater efficiency.

Charles Wiesenthal designed and received a patent on a double-pointed needle that eliminated the need to turn the needle around with each stitch. Other inventors of that time tried to develop a functional sewing machine, but each design had at least one serious flaw.

Frenchman Barthelemy Thimonnier finally engineered a machine that really worked. However, he was nearly killed by a group of angry tailors when they burned down his garment factory. They feared that they would lose their jobs to the machine.

American inventor Elias Howe received a patent for a method of sewing that used thread from two different sources. Howe's machine had a needle with an eye at the point, and it used the two threads to make a special stitch called a lockstitch. However, Howe faced difficulty in finding buyers for his machines in America. In frustration, he traveled to England to try to sell his invention there. When he finally returned home, he found that dozens of manufacturers were adapting his discovery for use in their own sewing machines.

Isaac Singer was also a manufacturer who made improvements to the design of sewing machines. He invented an up-and-down-motion mechanism that replaced the side-to-side machines. He also developed a foot *treadle* to power his machine. This improvement left the sewer's hands free. It was a huge improvement of the hand-cranked machine of the past. However, Singer used the same method to create a lockstitch that Howe had already patented. As a result, Howe sued him for patent infringement. Elias Howe won the court case, and Singer was ordered to pay Howe royalties. Howe became a millionaire, not by manufacturing the sewing machine, but by receiving royalty payments for his invention.

© Rainbow Bridge Publishing

Reading Comprehension

1. Why was Barthelemy Thimonnier's garment factory burned down?
   A. It did not have an adequate sprinkler system.
   B. Workers who feared the loss of their jobs to a machine burned the factory down.
   C. Oil used to lubricate the sewing machines was ignited by a careless smoker.
   D. Elias Howe felt that Thimonnier was trying to steal his invention.

2. Which of the following best defines the word *treadle*?
   A. a lever powered by the foot
   B. a power source from a unique type of extension cord
   C. a type of crude treadmill
   D. a looping mechanism near the eye of the needle

3. Which statement offers the best explanation for why the court forced Isaac Singer to pay Elias Howe a lifetime of royalties?
   A. The judge was biased against Singer for his surly attitude.
   B. Howe had already patented the lockstitch used by Singer.
   C. Singer had borrowed money from Howe and never repaid it.
   D. Singer and Howe had both invented the same machine.

4. Which of the following would be another good title for this reading?
   A. A Stitch in Time Saves Nine
   B. The Early History of the Sewing Machine
   C. Howe versus Singer
   D. Patent Laws

5. Elias Howe was unsuccessful at selling his sewing machine. Isaac Singer made many of his own improvements to the sewing machine. Singer was also a talented businessman, and he successfully marketed his improved machine. Eventually, after a battle in court, Singer paid Howe a $25.00 royalty for every machine that he sold. Do you think that this decision was fair? Explain your answer on a separate sheet of paper.

© Rainbow Bridge Publishing

Fireside Chats

On October 29, 1929, the United States stock market crashed. In the days that followed, banks and businesses closed, the number of unemployed workers rose to 15 million, and many people lost their savings. As the economic crisis wore on, it became known as the Great Depression. It left many people feeling anxious and uncertain about the future.

Within days of his inauguration in 1933, President Franklin Delano Roosevelt (FDR) began taking steps to stabilize the banking system, support the economy, and provide jobs for unemployed workers. To keep the American public informed about the changes that were underway, he gave a series of radio addresses called fireside chats. FDR used these broadcasts to speak about a number of issues. The first of Roosevelt's fireside chats was delivered on Sunday, March 12, 1933. His goal in this message was to explain the bank crisis in the United States.

He explained to Americans why banks had run out of money. Roosevelt assured people that their money was safe and that they could get their money when they really needed it. He said that most of the banks would be open the next day and that others would be open again very soon. His message's purpose was to restore Americans' confidence in their banking system.

Roosevelt's chats to America were popular with the people. Many looked forward to hearing what FDR had to say. The White House did not always tell the public whether a particular radio address was to be regarded as a fireside chat. As a result, there is some question about the exact number of these speeches. Twenty-eight such addresses were definitively identified, and two other radio addresses could have also been chats.

Roosevelt delivered his messages throughout much of the time that he was president. He delivered his final fireside chat on June 12, 1944. The focus was opening a fifth war-loan drive. He complimented the American people for supporting the war effort with the purchase of more than $32 billion of war bonds. He encouraged them to buy more as the war effort continued to cost money every day, money that he confidently predicted would lead to final victory.

© Rainbow Bridge Publishing

Reading Comprehension

1. Which of the following best explains Roosevelt's motives for delivering his fireside chats?
   A. to enhance his political image
   B. to keep the American public informed
   C. to help improve the Democratic cause in Congress
   D. to fulfill a promise that he had made to the public when he was running for president

2. How many definitively identified fireside chats did Roosevelt deliver to the American public?
   A. 4
   B. 12
   C. 24
   D. 28

3. What topic did FDR choose for his final fireside chat?
   A. war bonds
   B. the national debt
   C. the economy
   D. health care for all Americans

4. During which of the following time frames did Roosevelt deliver his messages?
   A. 1886—1891
   B. 1917—1924
   C. 1929—1939
   D. 1933—1944

5. Why do you think Roosevelt chose this forum for his addresses to the American people?

   _____

   _____

   _____

   _____

© Rainbow Bridge Publishing

Reading Comprehension • RB-904059

The Father of Medicine

Hippocrates was a physician who was born around 460 BC on the island of Cos, Greece. He believed that illness had both a physical and a rational explanation. This belief contrasted the accepted theory of the day. Most people believed that illness was caused by evil spirits and the disfavor of the gods.

Hippocrates treated the body as an entity, not as a series of unrelated parts. His prescription for good health included plenty of rest, a good diet, fresh air, and cleanliness. Hippocrates also approached medicine scientifically. He and those who followed his teachings made careful records of each case. Some of those observations remain true today. He was the first physician to describe the symptoms of pneumonia and of epilepsy in children.

Hippocrates had strong feelings about how doctors should behave. He founded a medical school and began teaching his ideas. There, he began incorporating his code of behavior for physicians into his teaching. His Oath of Medical Ethics for physicians became known as the Hippocratic Oath. It is one of the oldest binding documents in history.

Many of the Hippocratic Oath's principles are honored by doctors today. Most students graduating from medical school still swear to some form—usually a modernized version—of the oath. While the language has changed, its important principles remain much the same—doctors pledge to treat patients to the best of their abilities, honor the privacy of all patients, and teach medicine to the next generation.

Because of his contributions to medicine, Hippocrates has long been referred to as "The Father of Medicine."

                    Reading Comprehension • RB-904059

Reading Comprehension

1. Which of the following best explains the difference between the beliefs of Hippocrates and those that were popular in his day?
   A. Hippocrates believed that treatment should be free for those who could not afford to pay.
   B. Hippocrates thought that evil spirits should be tamed before recovery was possible.
   C. Hippocrates believed that there was a rational explanation for diseases and approached medicine scientifically.
   D. Hippocrates treated each part of the body separately.

2. Hippocrates' prescription for good health included all of the following except
   A. following a healthy diet.
   B. cleanliness.
   C. exercising regularly.
   D. getting plenty of rest.

3. Perhaps the greatest legacy of Hippocrates is
   A. his Oath of Medical Ethics.
   B. his prescription for good health.
   C. his compassion for patients who had no money.
   D. his proof that evil spirits played a role in medicine.

4. Which of the following events happened first?
   A. Hippocrates described the symptoms of pneumonia.
   B. Evil spirits and the disfavor of the gods were considered to be explanations for illness.
   C. Hippocrates developed an Oath of Medical Ethics for physicians.
   D. Hippocrates became recognized as "The Father of Medicine."

5. When it comes to health care, what is the number one quality that you want the physician who treats your illnesses to have? Why?

   _____

   _____

© Rainbow Bridge Publishing

GPS

GPS is the acronym for Global Positioning System. It is a method of pinpointing the exact location of any place on Earth. The system was originally developed by the United States government for use in the military. It is now used by everyone else, too.

The heart of the system is a series of 24 satellites that are orbiting high above Earth's surface. Each satellite makes two rotations around Earth every day. To use the GPS, a person must have a device that receives the high frequency radio signals that are sent out from the satellites. To determine its exact location, the receiver locates four or more of the satellites. It then calculates its distance from each of the satellites. By using the various distances, it finds the point where the distances intersect. That point is where the receiver and the person using it are located. This concept is called three-dimensional trilateration.

Each satellite is equipped with four atomic clocks that record the precise time when a signal is sent. Each receiver also has a clock that must be constantly reset to the exact time of the clocks in the satellite. The receiver measures the time it takes for the signal from the satellite to reach the receiver. It then multiplies this by the speed of light to determine the distance from which the signal came.

When the receiver has completed its calculations, it has determined the latitude, the longitude, and even the altitude of its position. The receiver then sends this data into map files found in its memory. This not only places the user on a detailed map, but, if the receiver is left on, it will also follow the user's path as he travels from one place to another.

© Rainbow Bridge Publishing

Reading Comprehension

1. The acronym *GPS* stands for
   A. Government Positioning Service.
   B. Global Positioning Service.
   C. Grade Positioning System.
   D. Global Positioning System.

2. Which of the following is not a function performed by a GPS device?
   A. It measures the distances of four or more satellites.
   B. It measures the amount of time between when signals are sent from a satellite and when they arrive at the receiver.
   C. It sends its recorded data to a series of stored maps to give the user a visual location.
   D. It has a tiny cell phone for use in emergencies and a built-in computer for receiving e-mails.

3. Handheld GPS receivers can calculate all of the following data except
   A. temperature.
   B. latitude.
   C. altitude.
   D. longitude.

4. Why is it necessary that at least four satellites must be located for GPS to be accurate?
   A. Two satellites are better than one.
   B. One satellite might not be working at the time.
   C. The receiver needs to pinpoint the intersection of the distances of at least four satellites.
   D. The GPS device needs to receive a signal from each of the four cardinal directions.

5. Other than to help a person know where she is at any given point in time, what other uses make GPS a helpful technology?

   _____

   _____

   _____

   _____

© Rainbow Bridge Publishing

Critical Thinking Skills

Analogies

Circle the letter in front of the answer that correctly completes each analogy.

1. Telescope is to microscope as star is to
   A. planet.
   B. glass.
   C. cell.
   D. universe.

2. Omniscient is to omnipotent as knowledge is to
   A. hope.
   B. power.
   C. fear.
   D. despair.

3. In is to import as out is to
   A. exit.
   B. export.
   C. exult.
   D. expose.

4. Assertive is to passive as definite is to
   A. certain.
   B. exact.
   C. define.
   D. vague.

5. Evil is to malevolent as good is to
   A. sullen.
   B. benevolent.
   C. relentless.
   D. villainous.

6. Reveal is to divulge as hide is to
   A. discover.
   B. imagine.
   C. conceal.
   D. inform.

7. Observe is to observation as condense is to
   A. condensed.
   B. condensation.
   C. respiration.
   D. information.

8. Piece is to fragment as daydream is to
   A. night.
   B. fatigue.
   C. boredom.
   D. reverie.

© Rainbow Bridge Publishing

Reading Comprehension • RB-904059

Critical Thinking Skills

Eponyms, Acronyms, and Portmanteau Words

Write the correct word and identify each answer as an eponym, an acronym, or a portmanteau word. **Remember:** An eponym is a name or a noun that is formed from the name of a person. Acronyms are words that are formed from the initial letters of other words. Portmanteau words blend the sounds and meanings of two words into a single new word.

America	Internet	brunch	sandwich
SCUBA	LASER	motel	RADAR

1. Light amplification by stimulation emission of radiation

   _____   _____

2. Self-contained underwater breathing apparatus

   _____   _____

3. Radio detecting and range

   _____   _____

4. From the name of Amerigo Vespucci, an explorer

   _____   _____

5. motor + hotel

   _____   _____

6. breakfast + lunch

   _____   _____

7. From the title, the fourth Earl of Sandwich

   _____   _____

8. international + network

   _____   _____

Reading Comprehension • RB-904059

Critical Thinking Skills

What's the Question?

Read the answers below. Then, on the line before each answer, write an appropriate question.

1. Q. _____

A. Fold several pages of newspaper or tissue paper around the flower. Place the wrapped flower within the pages of a heavy book, such as a dictionary or an encyclopedia. Change the paper once a week until the paper has absorbed all of the moisture from the flower.

2. Q. _____

A. Make sure the lamp or light fixture has been turned off. If the bulb is hot, allow it to cool. Grasp the bulb lightly but firmly. Turn the bulb counterclockwise until it is released from the socket. Carefully insert a replacement bulb into the socket. Turn it clockwise until it is snug.

3. Q. _____

A. Place your index and middle fingers firmly against the inside of your wrist. Once you feel a steady pulse, count the number of pulses for 10 seconds and multiply that number by six.

4. Q. _____

A. Avoid exposure to the sun between 10 A.M. and 3 P.M., when the sun's rays are most intense. At least 15 minutes before going outdoors, liberally apply sunblock with a sun protection factor of at least 15 to all exposed skin, including the ears, nose, neck, hands, feet, eyelids, and scalp. Wear a hat with at least a three-inch brim and sunglasses that block 100 percent of UVA and UBA rays. Seek shade.

© Rainbow Bridge Publishing

Reading Comprehension • RB-904059

Critical Thinking Skills

Oxymorons

An oxymoron is a figure of speech that is created when words with opposite or contradictory meanings are used together. For example, the phrase *jumbo shrimp* is an oxymoron, because the word *jumbo* means *large*, and the word *shrimp* is sometimes used to describe things that are very small. Underline the oxymoron in each of the sentences below. Then, on the line provided, explain why the phrase is contradictory.

1. The movie director reminded her actors to try to act naturally while the cameras were rolling.

   _____

2. To get his student identification badge, Troy had to have an original copy of his birth certificate.

   _____

3. I would like to have an exact estimate of how many people are coming to the party, so please remember to RSVP to the invitation.

   _____

4. For homework, the teacher asked each student to write a detailed summary of her favorite book.

   _____

5. The contestants performed in random order.

   _____

6. When the guest lecturer began to walk toward the podium, a deafening silence filled the auditorium.

   _____

Reading Comprehension • RB-904059

Critical Thinking Skills

Words from Greek and Latin Roots

Circle the letter in front of the correct meaning for each root. Then, on the lines provided, write two words that contain the root.

1. therm   A. above   B. heat   C. after

   _____   _____

2. anti   A. against   B. for   C. book

   _____   _____

3. morph   A. love   B. form   C. change

   _____   _____

4. biblio   A. form   B. good   C. book

   _____   _____

5. cardio   A. heart   B. measure   C. power

   _____   _____

6. bio   A. sea   B. far   C. life

   _____   _____

7. tri   A. one   B. two   C. three

   _____   _____

8. ology   A. study of   B. fear   C. all

   _____   _____

9. chron   A. time   B. fear   C. study of

   _____   _____

10. port   A. carry   B. out   C. in

    _____   _____

© Rainbow Bridge Publishing   *Reading Comprehension* • RB-904059

Critical Thinking Skills

Palindromes and Reflections

A palindrome is a word, phrase, or sentence that means the same thing when read either forward or backward. The word *eye* is an example of a palindrome. Think of all the palindromes you can and list them on the lines below. **Hint:** Try to think of words that begin and end with the same letter.

_____   _____   _____

_____   _____   _____

_____   _____   _____

_____   _____   _____

_____   _____   _____

Unlike a palindrome, a reflection forms a new word when it is spelled backward. The word *swap* is an example of a reflection; spelled backwards, it makes the word *paws*. Fill in the blanks below with the reflection that best fits each clue.

1. a storage place for clothes _____

   a sum offered for the detection of a criminal _____

2. a thin hollow tube used for drinking _____

   growths on the skin caused by a virus _____

3. another word for students _____

   a mistake or error _____

4. to correct something prior to publication _____

   the rising and falling of the sea _____

5. to move smoothly, as in water _____

   a wild dog that lives and hunts in a pack _____

Reading Comprehension • RB-904059

Critical Thinking Skills

Idioms

Use the clues to unscramble the idioms. Write the idioms on the lines.

1. There can be many ways of doing something.

   lead roads Rome all to

   _____

2. forced to decide between unpleasant choices

   and between hard rock a place a

   _____

3. unable to think of a word that you know

   of the tongue on tip your

   _____

4. to hear something and then immediately forget it

   the in out ear one other and

   _____

5. to accept more responsibility than you can handle

   chew more bite than can you off

   _____

6. If you want to be successful, don't procrastinate.

   catches bird worm the early the

   _____

7. If something is free, don't be too critical of it.

   in look horse the don't a gift mouth

   _____

Answer Key

Page 5, Gold-Medal Miracle
1. C.; 2. C.; 3. C.; 4. D.; 5. Answers will vary. The facts that the Soviet Union's team was composed entirely of professional athletes, while the U.S. team was composed of amateur athletes, and that the Soviet team had beaten the U.S. team badly in an exhibition game made the USSR an overwhelming favorite.

Page 7, It's Missouri's Fault
1. D.; 2. B.; 3. A.; 4. B.; 5. Answers will vary, but could include the following: adopt building codes to meet earthquake design standards; increase earthquake education in schools; create plans for earthquake preparedness, response, and recovery; and continue to monitor the fault line for seismic activity.

Page 9, The First Burger?
1. B.; 2. C.; 3. B.; 4. A.; 5. Answers will vary.

Page 11, Analyzing Poetry
1. B.; 2. D.; 3. Answers will vary but should include the idea that hope is most important during difficult times.; 4. soul/all, storm/warm; 5. Answers will vary but could include statements such as: The dashes make the reader pause in unusual places, and Dickinson's use of capitalization helps emphasize important words.

Pages 12–13, Fabulous Fables
Answers will vary. Possible answers include: 1. You can't be too small to make a difference. 2. Kindness can achieve greater results than force. 3. Goals can be achieved by taking many small steps. 4. Selfish behavior may lead to loss. 5. There is strength in unity.

Page 15, On the Mission Trail
1. B.; 2. B.; 3. B.; 4. D.; 5. It encouraged settlement and protected Spain's claims on the area. It also brought livestock, industry, and the cultivation of fruits, flowers, and grains to California.

Page 17, Seventh-Inning Stretch
1. C.; 2. B.; 3. C.; 4. C.; 5. Answers will vary.

Page 19, Sunshine in Seattle
1. D.; 2. D.; 3. A.; 4. B.

Page 21, The Last Spike
1. D.; 2. B.; 3. B.; 4. C.; 5. Answers will vary. Possible answers include: Passengers could travel to the West without fear of being ambushed, and the journey could be completed in days rather than months. Cattle and wheat could be shipped to eastern manufacturing cities.

© Rainbow Bridge Publishing

Answer Key

Page 23, And Now . . . the Weather!
1. B.; 2. D.; 3. C.; 4. B.; 5. Answers will vary.

Page 25, *Exxon Valdez*
1. C; 2. C; 3. C; 4. D; 5. Answers will vary.

Page 27, Affirmed by a Nose
1. C.; 2. C; 3. B; 4. B; 5. Answers will vary. It is difficult for a horse to win three separate races that require very different strengths and strategies.

Page 29, The First Lady of Song
1. C.; 2. 2, 1, 5, 4, 3; 3. B.; 4. Answers will vary.

Page 31, The Great Grocery Debate
1. C.; 2. They believe that eating genetically modified food may cause side effects that are not yet known. 3. Scientists can create new breeds of fruits and vegetables. Genetically modified foods may help feed the world's increasing population. 4. Answers will vary.

Page 33, About to Blow?
1. B.; 2. B.; 3. D.; 4. D.; 5. Answers will vary, but the newly discovered bulge on the bottom of Yellowstone Lake will probably not result in fewer visitors to the park.

Page 35, Why Sunsets Are Beautiful
1. A.; 2. C.; 3. A.; 4. C.; 5. The path of sunlight has a greater distance to travel when the sun is low in the sky.

Page 35, continued
Hence, the shorter blue wavelengths scatter and the longer wavelengths of the reds and oranges are what we see.

Page 37, Stuffed Love
1. C.; 2. B.; 3. B.; 4. D.; 5. Answers will vary, but someone probably would have thought of the idea eventually.

Page 39, Mystery of the *Maine*
1. D.; 2. A.; 3. B.; 4. B.; 5. Answers will vary.

Page 41, America's Aging Population
1. C.; 2. D.; 3. B.; 4. D.; 5. As people grow older, many lose their ability to drive cars. This can leave them isolated in their homes if there is no available public transportation.

Page 43, All Charged Up!
1. B.; 2. B.; 3. C.; 4. D.; 5. Answers will vary, but most likely the eel would shock a human being on contact.

Page 45, The Big Dance
1. C.; 2. B.; 3. B.; 4. C.; 5. Answers will vary.

Page 47, The Blarney Stone
1. C.; 2. C.; 3. C.; 4. C.; 5. Answers will vary.

Answer Key

Page 49, Hay-Fever Season
1. C.; 2. A.; 3. B.; 4. C.; 5. Avoid the pollens that cause a reaction if possible. Air conditioning and air-purifying systems may also lessen exposure. Antihistamines can reduce some of the symptoms as well.

Page 51, Garlic's Time
1. D.; 2. D.; 3. C.; 4. A.; 5. Many people do use garlic in their diets on a regular basis. However, some dislike its taste and others dislike the bad breath it causes in some people.

Page 53, Asteroids
1. D.; 2. A.; 3. A.; 4. B.; 5. Answers will vary. Issues included recognition of the threat, disaster preparedness, and techniques and technology to use in Earth's defense.

Page 55, Totem Poles
1. C.; 2. D.; 3. D.; 4. A.; 5. Answers will vary, but the beauty and craftsmanship of the totem poles were noticed by art and history lovers who worked to revive the lost art.

Page 57, A Rare Find
1. C.; 2. C.; 3. D.; 4. B.; 5. Answers will vary, but one of the factors in determining the value of a stamp is how rare it is. Other factors include the condition of the stamp and the story behind the stamp.

Page 59, The Great Wall
1. C.; 2. A.; 3. C.; 4. B.; 5. Answers will vary, but many historians think that it was built to keep out invaders from the north.

Page 61, First, the Lightning
1. C.; 2. C.; 3. D.; 4. A.; 5. Count the number of seconds between the flash of a lightning strike and the sound of the thunder. The number of seconds divided by five will be the distance in miles that you are from the lightning strike.

Page 63, Stitches
1. B.; 2. A.; 3. B.; 4. B.; 5. Answers will vary.

Page 65, Fireside Chats
1. B.; 2. D.; 3. A.; 4. D.; 5. Answers will vary. Radio was quite popular during this period of history. Many Americans were glued to their radios each evening, much in the same way that people watch television today.

Page 67, The Father of Medicine
1. C.; 2. C.; 3. A.; 4. B.; 5. Answers will vary.

Page 69, GPS
1. D.; 2. D.; 3. A.; 4. C.; 5. There are many uses of this technology currently on the market. They include distance and direction locators in automobiles, handheld models for hikers to prevent them from getting lost, to help locate stolen vehicles, to measure distances on a golf course, etc.

Answer Key

Page 70, Analogies
1. C.; 2. B.; 3. B.; 4. D.; 5. B.; 6. C.;
7. B; 8. D.

Page 71, Eponyms, Acronyms, and Portmanteau Words
1. LASER, acronym; 2. SCUBA, acronym; 3. RADAR, acronym; 4. America, eponym; 5. motel, portmanteau word; 6. brunch, portmanteau word; 7. sandwich, eponym; 8. Internet, portmanteau word

Page 72, What's the Question?
1. How do you preserve a flower?
2. How do you change a lightbulb?
3. How do you take your pulse?
4. How do you protect your skin from the sun?

Page 73, Oxymorons
1. act naturally, acting is not natural; 2. original copy, a copy is not an original; 3. exact estimate, an estimate is an inexact number; 4. detailed summary, summaries are short overviews without many details; 5. random order, an order is a specific arrangement; 6. deafening silence, deafening implies very loud noise, while silence is the absence of noise.

Page 74, Words from Greek and Latin Roots
Examples of words will vary.
1. B., thermostat, thermometer; 2. A., antibody, antifreeze; 3. C., metamorphosis, amorphous; 4. C. bibliography, bibliophile; 5. A., cardiovascular, cardiology; 6. C., biology, biosphere; 7. C., trifold, triceratops; 8. B., archaeology, biology; 9. A., chronology, synchronize; 10. A., transport, portable

Page 75, Palindromes and Reflections
Answers will vary. Possible answers include: bib, dad, deed, eye, gag, kayak, level, madam, mom, peep, pop, RADAR, racecar, redder, tat, wow; 1. drawer/reward; 2. straw/warts; 3. pupils/slipup; 4. edit/ tide; 5. flow/wolf

Page 76, Idioms
1. All roads lead to Rome.; 2. between a rock and a hard place; 3. on the tip of your tongue; 4. in one ear and out the other; 5. bite off more than you can chew; 6. the early bird catches the worm; 7. Don't look a gift horse in the mouth.

© Rainbow Bridge Publishing